NATURAL WONDERS OF THE WORLD

THE GRAND CANYON

by Rebecca Kraft Rector

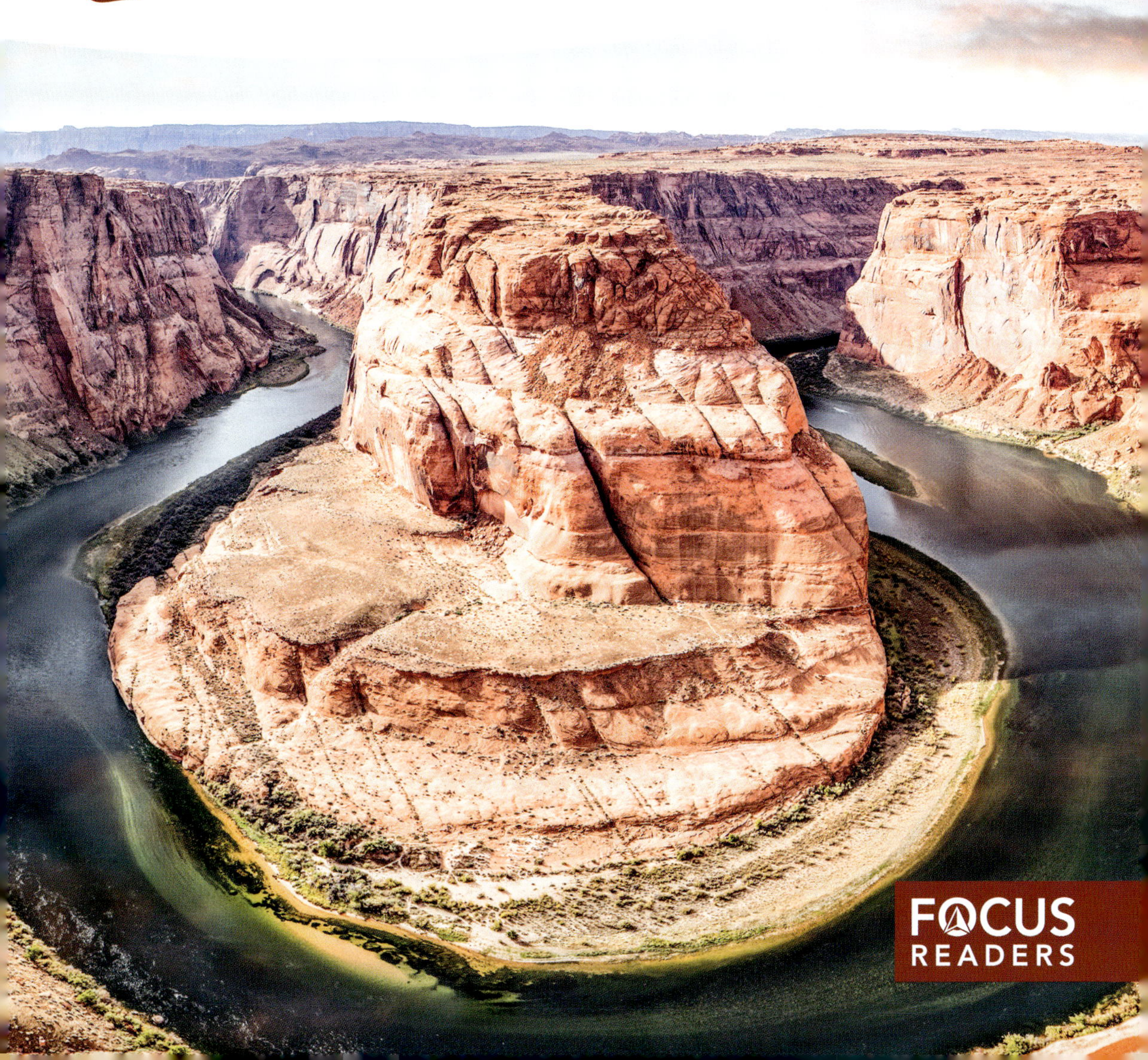

FOCUS READERS

www.focusreaders.com

Copyright © 2018 by Focus Readers, Lake Elmo, MN 55042. All rights reserved. No part of this book may be reproduced or utilized in any form or by any means without written permission from the publisher.

Focus Readers is distributed by North Star Editions:
sales@northstareditions.com | 888-417-0195

Produced for Focus Readers by Red Line Editorial.

Content Consultant: Jeffrey R. Walker, PhD, Professor of Earth Science, Vassar College

Photographs ©: MundusImages/iStockphoto, cover, 1; maislam/iStockphoto, 4–5; tonda/iStockphoto, 7, 12, 26; Red Line Editorial, 9, 21; julof90/iStockphoto, 10–11; jacknpushpa/iStockphoto, 15; Michael Quinn/Grand Canyon National Park, 17; MWKphoto/iStockphoto, 18–19; kojihirano/iStockphoto, 23; Bim/iStockphoto, 24–25; jose1983/iStockphoto, 29

ISBN
978-1-63517-513-4 (hardcover)
978-1-63517-585-1 (paperback)
978-1-63517-729-9 (ebook pdf)
978-1-63517-657-5 (hosted ebook)

Library of Congress Control Number: 2017948101

Printed in the United States of America
Mankato, MN
November, 2017

ABOUT THE AUTHOR

Rebecca Kraft Rector is a writer, librarian, and researcher. She is the author of novels, nonfiction books, and more than 100 nonfiction articles.

TABLE OF CONTENTS

CHAPTER 1
An Awesome View 5

CHAPTER 2
How the Grand Canyon Was Formed 11

IT'S A WONDER!
Ancient Remains 16

CHAPTER 3
Plants and Animals 19

CHAPTER 4
The Grand Canyon Today 25

Focus on the Grand Canyon • 30
Glossary • 31
To Learn More • 32
Index • 32

CHAPTER 1

AN AWESOME VIEW

The mountain lion rests in a shady cave. Outside in the sun, the temperature is 100 degrees Fahrenheit (38°C). In front of the cave, the Grand Canyon spreads out for miles. Striped rock walls plunge steeply downward. In other places, they flatten or rise to make peaks. The Colorado River runs swiftly far below.

The views from atop the Grand Canyon are vast.

The sun is setting. The heat of the day fades. A piece of red rock seems to slither away. It is a Grand Canyon rattlesnake. Mule deer and elk look for safe spots to spend the night. Before long, black scorpions, bats, and ringtail cats will come out of their hiding places. Soon the mountain lion will hunt its prey. Until then, the mule deer and elk are safe. Hundreds of animal and plant **species** live in the Grand Canyon. Some exist nowhere else in the world.

The Grand Canyon is an enormous valley. It is one of the largest canyons on the planet. The canyon lies in the northwest corner of Arizona. Stretching

The Grand Canyon has an endless number of areas to explore.

up to 18 miles (29 km) wide, it is approximately 1 mile (1.6 km) deep and 277 miles (446 km) long. It can even be seen from space.

The weather throughout the canyon varies. Some places can reach temperatures of 120 degrees Fahrenheit (49°C) in the summer. Other places may reach only the mid-70s (mid-20s°C). Some levels are dry, and some are wet. In the winter, heavy snow may fall at the

A SACRED PLACE

Local American Indian tribes believe the Grand Canyon is a sacred place. Some believe it is where their people began. It is their homeland. They pray and hold religious ceremonies at the canyon. Some Hopi clans believe their people first came out of a dome. The dome is in the canyon near the Little Colorado River. It is called *Sipapuni*.

upper levels. Several feet of snow are not unusual. Other levels may receive only light rain. These differences create various **habitats**. The habitats are home to many plants and animals.

MAP OF THE GRAND CANYON

CHAPTER 2

HOW THE GRAND CANYON WAS FORMED

Earth's surface is made up of huge plates. These plates move very slowly across a layer of melted rock. When the plates collide, they can create earthquakes and volcanoes. They can also create mountains.

Around 80 million years ago, a sea covered the area where the canyon is now.

The Grand Canyon's features developed over millions of years.

The Colorado River still runs at the bottom of the Grand Canyon.

Plates shifted approximately 65 million years ago. They pushed up the land. Then, approximately five million years ago, the Gulf of California opened. It was much lower than the canyon area. Streams flowed toward it. They joined and formed the Colorado River.

The swiftly moving river carried mud, sand, and gravel. Strong floodwaters pushed enormous boulders through the river. The fast water, along with the materials it carried, cut through the land. Over time, the river's cutting action created a canyon.

Earth's crust is made of many layers of rock. The top layers of the Grand Canyon were exposed to wind and rain. This caused **erosion**, which wore away the walls that the river had created. The erosion made the upper walls wider. The river washed away the eroded rock. This made the canyon even deeper. The erosion is still going on today.

Most of the Grand Canyon has bare rock walls. Colorful horizontal stripes in the rocks show a cross-section of Earth's crust. The rocks in each layer formed at different times and under different conditions. The top layers are the newest. The bottom layers are the oldest.

Granite makes pink stripes in the canyon's oldest rocks. The granite formed 1.8 billion years ago. It started as very hot liquid rock below Earth's crust. The green stripes are layers of shale. Shale formed 515 million years ago in a deep, muddy sea. Layers of limestone formed 340 million years ago in a warm, shallow ocean. They are stained red from iron.

Each horizontal stripe of rock in the Grand Canyon was formed during a different time period.

Sandstone layers make light-colored stripes. They formed 275 million years ago when the land was a desert. The youngest layer of rock is also limestone. It is mostly gray and formed 270 million years ago. This is the rock at the top, or rim, of the canyon.

IT'S A WONDER!

ANCIENT REMAINS

Ancient remains preserved in rock are called fossils. Fossils are found in the different layers of the Grand Canyon.

The granite layer was formed by high heat and pressure. There are no fossils there. Above the granite, some layers were underwater millions of years ago. These layers have fossils of underwater creatures. Coral and sea sponge fossils are found here. Fossils of ferns have also been discovered.

Sandstone from the desert layer contains fossil tracks. The tracks belong to reptiles, spiders, and insects.

Thousands of years ago, people lived in the Grand Canyon. Some of their spear points have been found. Their paintings have been discovered on cave walls. Experts do not agree about what the paintings mean. Small figures made of twigs have also been found. The figures are shaped like

This fossil was found in the Grand Canyon.

deer or bighorn sheep. These animals still live in the Grand Canyon today.

CHAPTER 3

PLANTS AND ANIMALS

The Grand Canyon has five habitats. The bottom habitat is beside the river. Willows and cottonwoods grow here. Rare plants such as the white-flowering redbud and the stream orchid can also be found.

Above the bottom level is the desert scrub habitat. The conditions here are very hot and dry. But some plants thrive.

Bighorn sheep watch over the Grand Canyon.

These include creosote bushes, ocotillos, sagebrush, cacti, and yuccas.

The third habitat is woodlands of pinyon pine and juniper. Higher up, the next habitat is ponderosa pine forests. The highest habitat is the **boreal forest** on the canyon rims. This habitat includes spruces and mountain ash. Lupines and perennial grasses grow here as well.

The Grand Canyon is also home to hundreds of animal species. Birds account for approximately 450 of these species. Many rare and **endangered** birds shelter here. More common birds such as eagles, hawks, and ravens also make their homes in the Grand Canyon.

GRAND CANYON HABITATS

The layers of the Grand Canyon create five unique habitats. Different species live in each one.

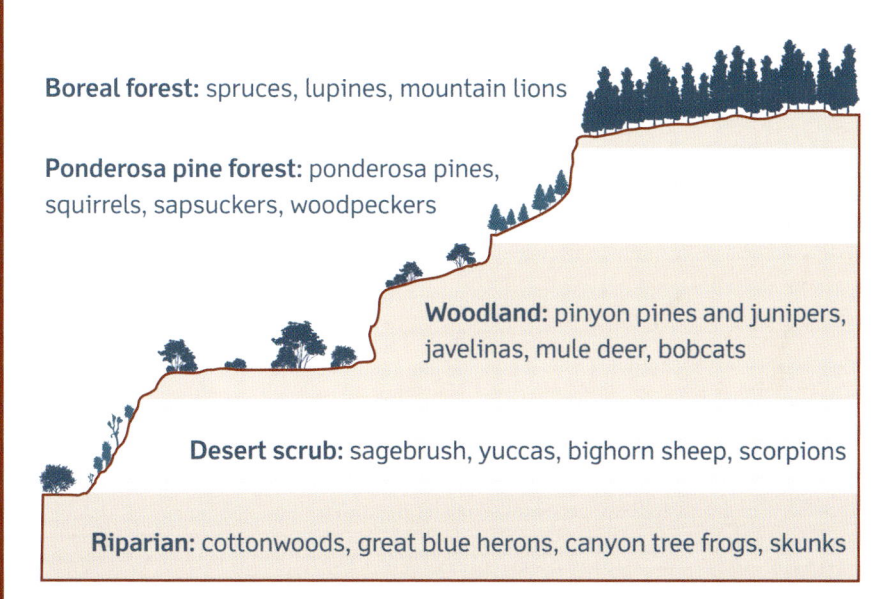

Boreal forest: spruces, lupines, mountain lions

Ponderosa pine forest: ponderosa pines, squirrels, sapsuckers, woodpeckers

Woodland: pinyon pines and junipers, javelinas, mule deer, bobcats

Desert scrub: sagebrush, yuccas, bighorn sheep, scorpions

Riparian: cottonwoods, great blue herons, canyon tree frogs, skunks

Ninety species of mammals live in the Grand Canyon. Mountain lions are the largest **predators** in the canyon. Bighorn sheep can be found in the desert scrub.

They also climb the rocky cliff sides. Twenty-two bat species live in the Grand Canyon. This is more than anywhere else in the United States. Other mammals include bobcats, mule deer, squirrels, and coyotes.

THE CALIFORNIA CONDOR

The California condor is the largest land bird in North America. It is also one of the rarest birds in the world. In 1982, there were only 22 California condors left on Earth. Scientists captured the birds to protect them. Slowly, their numbers grew. In 1996, six young birds were released in the Grand Canyon. By 2017, there were 500 wild condors. However, they are still endangered.

Scientists track the Grand Canyon's California condors by putting tracking tags under their wings.

Forty-one species of reptiles live throughout the canyon. Many live near the water and in desert scrub. Others live in the woodlands and forests. Lizards eat insects, and snakes eat rodents. Later, lizards and snakes become food for other animals. Gila monsters can be found in the desert scrub. Other reptiles include tortoises, salamanders, and toads.

CHAPTER 4

THE GRAND CANYON TODAY

The United States named the Grand Canyon a national monument in 1908. A portion of the canyon became a national park in 1919. But the Grand Canyon also has value to people around the world. In fact, it is one of the Seven Natural Wonders of the World.

More than six million people visited Grand Canyon National Park in 2016.

 Guides lead visitors around the Grand Canyon on mules.

Five American Indian tribes live in or near the Grand Canyon. The tribes are the Havasupai, Hopi, Hualapai, Navajo, and Paiute. The canyon plays a strong part in these tribes' traditions. The Havasupai farmed at the bottom of the canyon for centuries. They still have a village there.

Grand Canyon National Park has around five million visitors every year. They explore the canyon from the North Rim and South Rim. Visitors hike and camp. Daring people can go white-water rafting or skydive over the canyon. Others explore from planes or helicopters.

MULES OF THE CANYON

Mules have worked in the Grand Canyon since 1890. They carry equipment and people. They deliver the US mail to a Havasupai village. These sure-footed animals are carefully trained. They must handle miles of steep, narrow paths. Mules are generally smarter, stronger, and calmer than horses. The mules live in a barn on the South Rim.

The Grand Canyon faces threats. For instance, drought caused by climate change threatens the Colorado River. The upper part of the river is also used heavily for **irrigation**. As a result, the river's flow is very restricted by the time it reaches the Grand Canyon. Low water puts fish and wildlife in danger. Humans endanger the river in other ways. Dams change the river's flow. This affects habitats. Mining and power plants pollute the area.

Builders want to open new businesses at the canyon. This could cause more pollution. Some people oppose the businesses because they would be built on sacred American Indian land.

Preservation efforts are aiming to protect the Grand Canyon for generations to come.

People are working together to protect the canyon. The US government has passed new laws. A nearby power plant agreed to reduce its air pollution. Environmental groups also try to look after the canyon. In addition, American Indian tribes work hard to keep the Grand Canyon safe.

FOCUS ON
THE GRAND CANYON

Write your answers on a separate piece of paper.

1. Write a sentence that explains why the canyon walls are striped in different colors.

2. Would you like to ride a mule into the Grand Canyon? Why or why not?

3. Which habitat is on the canyon rims?

    A. woodlands
    B. desert scrub
    C. boreal forest

4. What might happen because of continuing erosion in the Grand Canyon?

    A. The stripes of color would disappear.
    B. The river would become bigger.
    C. The canyon would become deeper.

Answer key on page 32.

GLOSSARY

ancient
Very old.

boreal forest
A habitat where evergreen trees grow.

endangered
In danger of dying out.

erosion
The act of wearing away a surface.

habitats
The type of places where plants or animals normally grow or live.

irrigation
The redirecting of water to help crops grow.

predators
Animals that hunt other animals for food.

species
A group of animals or plants that are similar.

TO LEARN MORE

BOOKS

Chin, Jason. *Grand Canyon*. New York: Roaring Brook, 2017.

Mattern, Joanne. *The Grand Canyon: This Place Rocks*. Egremont, MA: Red Chair Press, 2017.

O'Connor, Jim. *Where Is the Grand Canyon?* New York: Grosset & Dunlap, 2015.

WEBSITES

Visit **www.focusreaders.com** to find lesson plans, activities, links, and other resources related to this title.

INDEX

American Indians, 8, 26, 28, 29

bighorn sheep, 17, 21
birds, 20, 22

California condor, 22
climate change, 28
Colorado River, 5, 12, 28
conservation, 29

earthquakes, 11
erosion, 13

fossils, 16

Grand Canyon National Park, 25, 27

habitats, 9, 19–20, 28
Havasupai, 26, 27
Hopi, 8, 26
Hualapai, 26

mammals, 21–22
mountain lions, 5, 6, 21
mule deer, 6, 22
mules, 27

Navajo, 26

Paiute, 26
plants, 19–20
plates, 11, 12

reptiles, 23
rock layers, 13–15, 16

Sipapuni, 8

volcanoes, 11

weather, 8–9

Answer Key: 1. Answers will vary; 2. Answers will vary; 3. C; 4. C